D1442713

PAUL & JEANNE RANKIN

Photography by SIMON WHEELER

THE MASTER CHEFS

TED SMART

PAUL AND JEANNE RANKIN have travelled together through Asia, experiencing at first hand many of the cuisines which make extensive use of chillies and spices. They learned the classical culinary skills at Le Gavroche, Albert Roux's renowned London restaurant, and then worked in a number of restaurants in Canada and the USA, culminating in a period in the Napa Valley, California, where Paul was executive chef and Jeanne was head pastry chef at the award-winning Mount View Hotel, Calistoga.

In 1989 they returned to Northern Ireland, Paul's birthplace, and opened their own restaurant, Roscoff, in Belfast; it became the first restaurant in Northern Ireland to be awarded a Michelin star, in 1991.

Their 15-part TV series, *Gourmet Ireland*, was shown throughout Ireland and the UK in 1994, and has also been screened in the USA and Canada, Australia, New Zealand, Hong Kong and Japan. There have since been two more series, accompanied by the books *Gourmet Ireland 1* and *2*.

Their first collection of spicy recipes, *Hot Food Cool Jazz*, was published in 1994, and, amazingly, they have also found time to appear on *Ready Steady Cook* for BBC 2 and *Curious Cooks* for BBC Radio 4.

Photograph by James Merrell

CONTENTS

A recipe is not meant to be followed exactly — it is a canvas on which you can embroider. Improvise and invent. Add the zest of this, a drop or two of that, a tiny pinch of the other. Let yourself be led by your palate and your tongue, your eyes and your heart. In other words, be guided by your love of food, and then you will be able to cook.

ROGER VERGÉ (*CUISINE OF THE SUN*, MACMILLAN LONDON, 1979)

INTRODUCTION

As far as Paul can remember, he has always enjoyed spicy food. First curry, then chilli con carne, then chicken noodle soup with lashings of chilli sauce. Some of his friends thought him rather odd, for they preferred cooler, blander fare. This makes us wonder just what is the influencing factor here? Is it climate, is it personality, or perhaps just human nature?

Most of the world enjoys food with a hefty dose of spices – think how the various cuisines tease the tastebuds. With the increase in international travel, communications and cross-cultural immigration, we in Britain are learning to enjoy the heat factor much more. For example, look at the inroads Thai and Mexican food have made. This suggests that it is indeed in our human nature to enjoy the sensations of culinary heat.

Our selection of recipes shows a global breadth of flavours. The carpaccio of salmon is not really Italian, as the name suggests, but a flat version of ceviche, that classic Mexican/South American dish of freshly marinated fish, enhanced with a good bit of chilli. The chicken puffs were born from an incorrigible fondness for sausage rolls with brown sauce...try them to see what we mean.

CHILLI CHICKEN PUFFS
with spicy dipping sauce

200 G/7 OZ CHICKEN FILLET,
   ROUGHLY CHOPPED
150 G/5 OZ STREAKY BACON,
   ROUGHLY CHOPPED
1 GARLIC CLOVE, FINELY CHOPPED
2 SPRING ONIONS, FINELY CHOPPED
2 TABLESPOONS CHOPPED FRESH
   CORIANDER
1 FRESH GREEN CHILLI, CHOPPED
1 EGG
½ TEASPOON SALT
½ TEASPOON PEPPER
A LITTLE FLOUR
1 PACKET (300–350 G/11–13 OZ)
   FROZEN PUFF PASTRY
1 EGG YOLK, BEATEN
2 TABLESPOONS BLACK AND WHITE
   SESAME SEEDS

TO SERVE

SPICY DIPPING SAUCE (PAGE 29)

MAKES ABOUT 24

Place the chicken and bacon in a
food processor with the garlic,
spring onions, coriander, chilli, egg,
salt and pepper. Pulse until the
mixture is well chopped and comes
together like sausage meat. Transfer
to a piping bag fitted with a
1½ cm/⅝ inch nozzle.

On a lightly floured surface, roll
out the pastry to about 3 mm/
⅛ inch thick. Cut the pastry into
strips about 6 cm/2½ inches wide.

Pipe the sausage meat along the
pastry strips. Lightly brush one
edge with egg yolk, then fold the
pastry over the meat and press
gently to seal; do not seal the ends.
Brush the top of the pastry with
egg yolk and sprinkle with the
sesame seeds. Cut into 6 cm/
2½ inch lengths and chill for 15
minutes. Preheat the oven to
200°C/400°F/Gas Mark 6.

Bake the puffs for 10 minutes
or until well risen and brown.
Reduce the oven temperature to
150°C/300°F/Gas Mark 3 and
cook for a further 10 minutes.

Serve warm, accompanied by
the dipping sauce.

CURRY AND COCONUT SOUP

1 TABLESPOON BUTTER

1 ONION, CHOPPED

1 GARLIC CLOVE, CHOPPED

2.5 CM/1 INCH PIECE OF FRESH
GINGER, CHOPPED

2 TABLESPOONS HOT (MADRAS)
CURRY POWDER

2 X 300 G/11 OZ CANS OF
SWEETCORN, DRAINED

600 ML/1 PINT CHICKEN STOCK

1 X 400 ML/14 FL OZ CAN OF
COCONUT MILK

SALT

TO SERVE

2 TABLESPOONS GREEK YOGURT

1 TEASPOON GARAM MASALA

OPTIONAL CONDIMENTS (PAGE 28)

SERVES 4–6

Melt the butter in a saucepan over low heat and sweat the onion, garlic and ginger until soft. Add the curry powder and cook for a further 2 minutes. Add the sweetcorn, chicken stock, coconut milk and a little salt. Simmer for 10 minutes.

Purée the soup in a liquidizer until smooth. If you prefer a more rustic texture, purée just half of the soup and stir back into the pan.

To serve, ladle the soup into warmed bowls, top with a swirl of the yogurt and a dusting of garam masala. Pass the condiments separately on a tray.

SPICED BEAN CURD
with a sesame and ginger vinaigrette

450 G/1 LB FRESH BEAN CURD
  (TOFU)
3 TABLESPOONS PLAIN FLOUR,
  SIFTED
3 TABLESPOONS SESAME SEEDS
1 TABLESPOON CHILLI POWDER
1 TABLESPOON WHITE PEPPER
2 TABLESPOONS ONION SALT
1 EGG, BEATEN WITH
  3 TABLESPOONS MILK
500 ML/16 FL OZ VEGETABLE OIL,
  FOR FRYING

TO SERVE

3 HEADS OF LITTLE GEM LETTUCE,
  SHREDDED
SESAME AND GINGER VINAIGRETTE
  (PAGE 30)
FRESH CORIANDER AND CHIVES

SERVES 4–6 AS A STARTER

Cut the bean curd into wedges, 2 cm/¾ inch thick. Mix the flour, sesame seeds, chilli powder, pepper and onion salt in a wide bowl. Dip each piece of bean curd lightly into the flour, then dip it into the egg and milk mixture and finally into the flour again.

Heat the oil in a wide pan to about 180°C/350°F or until a cube of bread browns in 30 seconds. Fry the bean curd for about 2 minutes on each side, until golden brown. Drain on paper towels.

To serve, pile the shredded lettuce on each plate and top with 3–4 pieces of bean curd. Sprinkle some of the vinaigrette over and around the bean curd. Garnish with the coriander and chives and serve at once.

GOATS' CHEESE FRITTERS
with Jalapeño chillies

325 G/12 OZ FRESH GOATS' CHEESE

1 SMALL JAR (ABOUT 175 G/6 OZ
OR SMALLER) SLICED JALAPEÑO
CHILLIES

A LITTLE FLOUR

125 G/4 OZ GROUND ALMONDS

125 G/4 OZ DRIED BREADCRUMBS

1 TABLESPOON CHOPPED FRESH
PARSLEY

1 EGG, BEATEN WITH 2
TABLESPOONS MILK

1 SMALL JAR (ABOUT 200 G/7 OZ)
ROASTED RED PEPPERS
(PIMENTOS)

100 ML/3½ FL OZ VINAIGRETTE

1 TEASPOON CHILLI SAUCE

VEGETABLE OIL FOR DEEP-FRYING

TO SERVE

BUNCH OF ROCKET

ROUGHLY CHOPPED CHIVES AND
TOASTED PINE NUTS (OPTIONAL)

SERVES 4

Using a small knife, remove the
skin from the goats' cheese. Drain
1–2 tablespoons of the chillies –
depending on how hot you like
your food – and pat them very dry
on paper towels. Place the cheese
and chillies in a food processor and
pulse for about 15 seconds or until
the cheese softens slightly. Tip the
mixture on to a clean surface and
divide it into 12 pieces. Sprinkle
lightly with flour and roll between
your hands to form perfect balls.

Mix together the almonds,
breadcrumbs and parsley. Dip each
cheese ball into the egg and milk
mixture and then into the almond
and breadcrumb mixture.
Refrigerate for at least 2 hours,
until they are quite firm.

Drain any excess liquid from
the pimentos and chop finely to
form a rough purée. Stir in the
vinaigrette and chilli sauce. Taste
and adjust the seasoning.

Heat the oil to 180°C/350°F
or until a cube of bread browns in
30 seconds. Fry the cheese balls
until just golden (don't fry them
too long or they will burst).

Arrange a bed of rocket on four
plates and spoon a generous
portion of the pimento vinaigrette
around the plate. Place the cheese
fritters on the rocket and serve at
once, garnished with chives and
toasted pine nuts.

CARPACCIO OF SALMON
with avocado, lime and fresh coriander

275 G/10 OZ FRESH SALMON
    FILLET
125 ML/4 FL OZ FRESH LIME JUICE
1 TEASPOON GRATED LIME ZEST
SALT AND PEPPER
2 FRESH CHILLIES, THINLY SLICED
1 SMALL RED ONION, FINELY
    CHOPPED
2 PLUM TOMATOES, SKINNED AND
    DICED
1 RIPE AVOCADO, FINELY DICED
4 TABLESPOONS EXTRA VIRGIN
    OLIVE OIL
2 TABLESPOONS ROUGHLY CHOPPED
    FRESH CORIANDER

SERVES 4

Trim the salmon of any brown meat and check for any bones, which should be removed with tweezers or small pliers. Using a long sharp knife, cut the salmon into 12 thin slices. Lay each slice in turn on some lightly oiled clingfilm or greaseproof paper, fold the paper over the fish and then, using a small rolling pin or cleaver, lightly flatten each slice so that it is very thin and even. Arrange the slices of salmon completely flat on four plates.

Reserving 1 tablespoon of the lime juice, whisk the remainder with the zest and 1 teaspoon salt, then add the chillies and chopped onion. Divide this lime mixture between the four plates, spreading it evenly over the salmon. Leave to marinate for 10–15 minutes.

When you are ready to serve, season the diced tomatoes and avocado with a little salt and pepper and toss in the reserved lime juice and olive oil. Divide between the four plates, sprinkle with the chopped coriander and serve at once.

COD WITH A PEANUT CRUST

1 ROUNDED TABLESPOON PEANUT
   BUTTER

1 EGG

1 TABLESPOON SOY SAUCE

1 TEASPOON GROUND GINGER

1 TABLESPOON FINELY CHOPPED
   ONION

50 G/2 OZ SALTED PEANUTS,
   CHOPPED

4 ROUNDED TABLESPOONS DRIED
   BREADCRUMBS

4 BONELESS COD FILLETS, ABOUT
   175 G/6 OZ EACH

SALT AND WHITE PEPPER

1 TABLESPOON VEGETABLE OIL

1 TABLESPOON BUTTER

SAUCE

2 TABLESPOONS OYSTER SAUCE

1 TABLESPOON SOY SAUCE

1 TABLESPOON SWEET SHERRY

1 TABLESPOON RICE WINE VINEGAR

1 TEASPOON SUGAR

1 TEASPOON DRIED CHILLI FLAKES

TO SERVE

1 BUNCH OF BOK CHOY OR
   CHINESE CABBAGE

FRESH CORIANDER AND SLICED
   SPRING ONIONS

SERVES 4

In a shallow bowl, whisk together the peanut butter, egg, soy sauce, ginger and onion until very smooth. Mix the chopped peanuts and the breadcrumbs together on a plate. Season the cod fillets with salt and pepper. Dip one side of each fillet into the peanut paste and then into the crumb mixture.

Heat the oil and butter in a frying pan until the butter foams, then add the cod fillets, crumb side down. Cook over moderate heat for about 4 minutes or until the crumbs are golden brown. Carefully turn the fish over and cook for about another 5 minutes, depending on how thick it is.

Stir together all the ingredients for the sauce.

Cook the bok choy in boiling salted water for 30 seconds, then drain well.

To serve, divide the bok choy between four warmed plates and surround with a little of the sauce. Carefully place a cod fillet on each plate and sprinkle with the coriander and spring onions.

SPAGHETTINI WITH PRAWNS,
rocket and chilli

450 G/1 LB SPAGHETTINI

175 ML/6 FL OZ EXTRA VIRGIN
  OLIVE OIL

450 G/1 LB FRESH PRAWNS, PEELED

SALT AND PEPPER

½ TEASPOON DRIED CHILLI FLAKES

2 TEASPOONS CHOPPED GARLIC

125 ML/4 FL OZ DRY WHITE WINE

1 TABLESPOON FRESH LEMON JUICE

SMALL BUNCH OF ROCKET

SERVES 4–6

Bring a large saucepan of salted water to a vigorous boil. Add the pasta and cook until *al dente* (just firm to the bite), about 6 minutes.

While the pasta is cooking, heat a large sauté pan over high heat until very hot. Add 3 tablespoons of the olive oil and then add the prawns. Season with salt and pepper and the chilli flakes. After about 1 minute, the prawns will turn pink; at this stage, add the garlic. Cook for another 30 seconds and then add the wine, lemon juice and 4 tablespoons water. When the wine boils vigorously, remove the pan from the heat.

When the pasta is done, drain well and toss with the remaining olive oil, the prawns and the rocket. Serve on individual warmed plates.

BREAST OF DUCK WITH HONEY
and Chinese five-spice

4 BARBARY DUCK BREASTS, ABOUT
175 G/6 OZ EACH

SALT

1 TEASPOON CHINESE FIVE-SPICE
POWDER

2 TABLESPOONS HONEY

4 TABLESPOONS JAPANESE SOY
SAUCE

2 TABLESPOONS BALSAMIC VINEGAR

A GOOD PINCH OF DRIED CHILLI
FLAKES

2 TABLESPOONS PICKLED GINGER,
CUT INTO THIN STRIPS

ABOUT 225 G/8 OZ EACH OF
CARROTS AND PARSNIPS, CUT
INTO STRIPS AND STEAMED OR
LIGHTLY BOILED

TO GARNISH
3–4 SPRING ONIONS, SLICED

SERVES 4

Trim the duck breasts and lightly
score the skin side with a sharp
knife. Season each breast lightly
with salt. Heat a large frying pan
over moderate heat and add the
duck breasts, skin side down. Cook
for about 5 minutes or until the
skin is an even golden colour. Turn
the breasts over and cook for about
another 2–3 minutes for medium-
rare duck.

In a small bowl, mix together
the five-spice powder, honey, soy
sauce, vinegar, chilli flakes and
pickled ginger.

Turn the duck breasts back to
their skin side down and pour off
any excess fat. Turn the heat up to
high and add the carrot and
parsnip strips. Sear for about 1
minute, then add the soy and
honey mixture. Let it bubble
furiously until it glazes the
vegetables and the duck.

Serve at once, on individual
warmed plates, sprinkled with
spring onions.

ROAST LEG OF LAMB
with cumin, lemon and mint

1 BONELESS LAMB JOINT, ABOUT
  800 G/1¾ LB
SALT
2 TABLESPOONS LIGHT OLIVE OIL
1 TEASPOON TOMATO PURÉE
1 TABLESPOON MINT SAUCE
1½ TABLESPOONS COLD BUTTER,
  CUT INTO SMALL PIECES

MARINADE

2 TEASPOONS GROUND CUMIN
1 TEASPOON GROUND BLACK
  PEPPER
1 TEASPOON HARISSA OR CHILLI
  AND GARLIC SAUCE
½ TEASPOON GROUND CORIANDER
  SEEDS
½ TEASPOON OREGANO
1 GARLIC CLOVE, CHOPPED, OR
  ¼ TEASPOON GARLIC POWDER
GRATED ZEST OF 1 LEMON
JUICE OF ½ LEMON

SERVES 4

Season the lamb generously with salt. Combine all the marinade ingredients in a shallow bowl. Dip the lamb into the marinade and rub the mixture into the meat. Leave to marinate for at least 30 minutes, preferably 2–3 hours, turning the meat occasionally.

Preheat the oven to 180°C/ 350°F/Gas Mark 4.

Heat the olive oil in a large frying pan over medium-high heat. Brown the lamb on all sides, then transfer to a warmed casserole dish. Add 2 tablespoons water and any remaining marinade and roast for about 20 minutes for medium-rare, 35 minutes for well-done lamb.

Transfer the roast to a warmed plate and cover with foil. Leave to rest in a warm place for 10 minutes. Pour the juices from the casserole into a small saucepan. Add the tomato purée and the mint sauce. Bring to the boil, then remove from the heat and whisk in the butter. Carve the roast and add any juices to the sauce. Serve with grilled Mediterranean vegetables: tomatoes, courgettes, aubergine.

RUMP STEAK WITH SOY AND GINGER

and chilli onion rings

4 WELL-AGED RUMP STEAKS, EACH
175–225 G/6–8 OZ AND ABOUT
2 CM/¾ INCH THICK

3 TABLESPOONS VEGETABLE OIL

MARINADE

4 TABLESPOONS JAPANESE SOY
SAUCE

4 TABLESPOONS MUSHROOM SOY
SAUCE

1 TABLESPOON GRATED FRESH
GINGER

2 TABLESPOONS SESAME OIL

1 TABLESPOON CURRY POWDER

CHILLI ONION RINGS

2–3 ONIONS

SALT

VEGETABLE OIL FOR DEEP-FRYING

300 G/11 OZ PLAIN FLOUR

2 TABLESPOONS CHILLI POWDER

2 TABLESPOONS PAPRIKA

2 TABLESPOONS CUMIN

SERVES 4

Combine all the marinade
ingredients in a ceramic dish. Add
the steaks and leave to marinate for
at least 30 minutes, preferably 2
hours, turning occasionally.

Using a very sharp knife or a
vegetable slicer, slice the onions
about 2 mm/¹⁄₁₆ inch thick.
Sprinkle lightly with salt and leave
to stand for 2–3 minutes.

Remove the steaks from the
marinade and pat dry, reserving the
marinade. Heat the oil in a large
frying pan and, when it is smoking,
add the steaks. Cook for 2 minutes
on each side for rare and about 4
minutes for medium. When the
steaks are cooked, transfer them to
a warmed plate and add the
reserved marinade to the pan. Boil
until it reduces to form a thickish
sauce. Keep warm.

To cook the onions, heat the
oil for deep-frying to about
170°C/340°F. Mix together the
flour, chilli powder, paprika and
cumin. Toss the onion slices in the
spiced flour and ensure that they
are evenly coated. Shake off excess
flour and deep-fry until brown and
crisp. Drain thoroughly on paper
towels and season with a little salt.

Arrange the steaks on four
warmed plates and spoon the sauce
over. Top with the chilli onion
rings and serve at once.

THE BASICS

CONDIMENTS

In those parts of the world where spicy hot food is eaten every day, it is
not uncommon to be offered a selection of accompaniments, which can be
added to the main dish to make it hotter, cooler, sweeter, crunchier, or
simply more colourful. Here is a selection of our favourites, which we
would serve as optional garnishes to our Curry and Coconut Soup.

COOKED PEELED PRAWNS

SHREDDED COOKED CHICKEN

SLICED SPRING ONIONS

CHOPPED FRESH CORIANDER

CHOPPED FRESH GREEN CHILLIES

CHILLI SAUCE

TOASTED COCONUT FLAKES

SOAKED RAISINS

CROÛTONS OF TOASTED NAAN BREAD

SPICY DIPPING SAUCE

1 TABLESPOON RICE WINE VINEGAR
1 TABLESPOON SUGAR
1½–3 TABLESPOONS CHILLI SAUCE
2 TEASPOONS FINELY CHOPPED
GARLIC
1 TEASPOON WHITE PEPPER
3 TABLESPOONS WORCESTERSHIRE
SAUCE
100 ML/3½ FL OZ FRESH ORANGE
JUICE
½ TEASPOON SALT
3 SPRING ONIONS, FINELY SLICED

Place all the ingredients in a small bowl and whisk with a fork.

It should be quite a hot sauce, because only tiny amounts are used as a dip, but since chilli sauce varies quite widely, don't put the whole quantity in at once – you can always add more, according to your own taste.

It can be stored in an airtight container in the refrigerator for up to 1 week.

SESAME GINGER VINAIGRETTE

1 TABLESPOON FINELY CHOPPED
   PICKLED GINGER
4 TABLESPOONS RICE WINE VINEGAR
4 TABLESPOONS DARK SOY SAUCE
2 TEASPOONS CHILLI SAUCE
4 TABLESPOONS SESAME OIL
6 TABLESPOONS SUNFLOWER OIL

Place all the ingredients in a small bowl and whisk together.

The vinaigrette can be stored in an airtight container in the refrigerator for up to 1 week. Whisk again before serving.

THE MASTER CHEFS

SOUPS
ARABELLA BOXER

MEZE, TAPAS AND ANTIPASTI
AGLAIA KREMEZI

PASTA SAUCES
GORDON RAMSAY

RISOTTO
MICHELE SCICOLONE

SALADS
CLARE CONNERY

MEDITERRANEAN
ANTONY WORRALL THOMPSON

VEGETABLES
PAUL GAYLER

LUNCHES
ALASTAIR LITTLE

COOKING FOR TWO
RICHARD OLNEY

FISH
RICK STEIN

CHICKEN
BRUNO LOUBET

SUPPERS
VALENTINA HARRIS

THE MAIN COURSE
ROGER VERGÉ

ROASTS
JANEEN SARLIN

WILD FOOD
ROWLEY LEIGH

PACIFIC
JILL DUPLEIX

CURRIES
PAT CHAPMAN

HOT AND SPICY
PAUL AND JEANNE RANKIN

THAI
JACKI PASSMORE

CHINESE
YAN-KIT SO

VEGETARIAN
KAREN LEE

DESSERTS
MICHEL ROUX

CAKES
CAROLE WALTER

COOKIES
ELINOR KLIVANS

THE MASTER CHEFS

This edition produced for The Book People Ltd,

Hall Wood Avenue, Haydock, St Helens WA11 9UL

Text © copyright 1996 Paul and Jeanne Rankin

Paul and Jeanne Rankin have asserted their right to
be identified as the Authors of this Work.

Photographs © copyright 1996 Simon Wheeler

First published in 1996 by

WEIDENFELD & NICOLSON

THE ORION PUBLISHING GROUP

ORION HOUSE

5 UPPER ST MARTIN'S LANE

LONDON WC2H 9EA

All rights reserved. No part of this publication may be
reproduced, stored in a retrieval system, or
transmitted in any form or by any means, electronic,
mechanical or otherwise, without prior permission of
the copyright holder.

British Library Cataloguing-in-Publication data
A catalogue record for this book is available
from the British Library.

ISBN 0 297 83643 9

DESIGNED BY THE SENATE

EDITOR MAGGIE RAMSAY

FOOD STYLIST JOY DAVIES

ASSISTANT KATY HOLDER